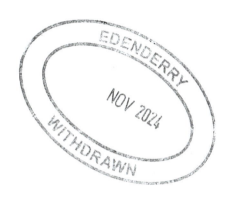

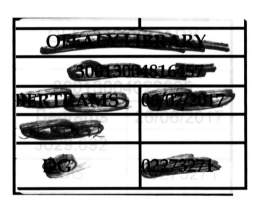

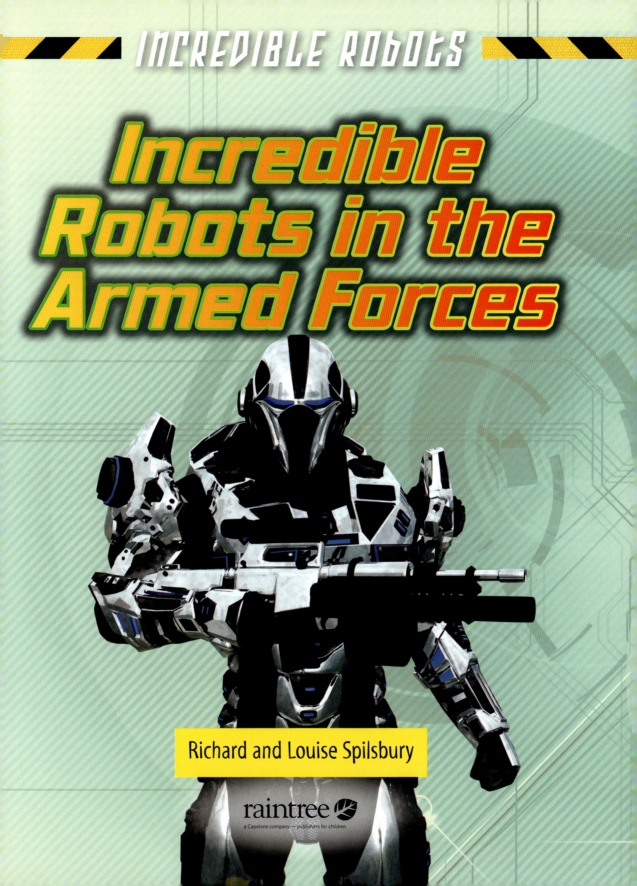

# Incredible Robots in the Armed Forces

Richard and Louise Spilsbury

raintree
a Capstone company — publishers for children

Raintree is an imprint of Capstone Global Library Limited, a company incorporated in England and Wales having its registered office at 264 Banbury Road, Oxford OX2 7DY – Registered company number: 6695582

**www.raintree.co.uk**
myorders@raintree.co.uk

Produced for Raintree by Calcium
Edited by Sarah Eason and Amanda Learmonth
Designed by Simon Borrough
Picture research by Susannah Jayes
Production by Victoria Fitzgerald
Originated by Capstone Global Library Ltd © 2016
Printed and bound in China

ISBN 978 1 4747 3126 3
20 19 18 17 16
10 9 8 7 6 5 4 3 2 1

**British Library Cataloguing in Publication Data**
A full catalogue record for this book is available from the British Library.

**Acknowledgements**
We would like to thank the following for permission to reproduce photographs: Dreamstime: Alexsalcedo 7, Sunsetman 6; Lockheed Martin Advanced Technology Laboratories 31; Shutterstock: Ivan Cholakov 35, DarkGeometryStudios 1, 40, Kevin Day 12, Digital Storm 4, Gkuna 17, Stefan Holm 30, Jarp2 27, E. Kryzhanivskyi 9, Mechanik 32, symbiot 15, Oleg Zabielin 26; US Department of Defense: Army Sgt. Matthew Acosta, 22 MPAD Fort Bragg, N.C. 13, Mass Communication Specialist 2nd Class Elizabeth R. Allen 10, PFC Pedro Amador 45, Technical Sgt. James L. Harper 36, Master Sgt. Steve Horton 37, Cpl. Bryan Nygaard 14, Sgt. Jennifer Pirante 11, Sgt. Brent C. Powell 29b, Senior Airman Julianne Showalater 8; US Navy: 23, Mass Communications Specialist 2nd Class Benjamin Crossley 18, Mass Communications Specialist Joe Kane 22, Photographer's Mate 1st Class Gregory Messier 21, John F. Williams 24; Wikimedia Commons: Bluefin Robotics Corporation/ Mierlo 25, Brennanphillips 19, DARPA 44, Hpeterswald 43tr, Tactical Technology Office, Defense Advanced Research Projects Agency 16, US Army 5, US Army Program Executive Office Soldier 41, 42, US Department of Defense/Tech Sgt. Russell E. Cooley IV, US Air Force 28, US Department of Defense/Sgt. Jason Dangel 34, US Department of Defense/Sgt. 1st Class Michael Guillory 29t, US Navy/Mass Communications Specialist Seaman Leonard Adams 43b, US Navy/Capt. Jane E. Campbell 39, US Navy/Alan Radecki 33, US Navy/Mass Communications Specialist 2nd Class Timothy Walter 38, US Navy/Photographer's Mate 1st Class Daniel N. Woods 20.

Cover photographs reproduced with permission of: Shutterstock: Daseaford (fg), Simon_G (bg).

Design Elements by Shutterstock; nice monkey, (stripes) throughout, phipatbig, (robot) throughout, vlastas, (tech background) throughout.

# Contents

Chapter 1 ............................. 4
Robot armies

Chapter 2 ............................. 12
Heavy-duty bots

Chapter 3 ............................. 18
Underwater bots

Chapter 4 ............................. 26
Flying mini-bots

Chapter 5 ............................. 32
Robot air force

Chapter 6 ............................. 40
Robot soldiers

Glossary ............................. 46

Find out more ....................... 47

Index ................................. 48

# Chapter 1

# Robot armies

When we watch films about battles set in the future, these conflicts are often being waged by robots and other machines that fight instead of, or alongside, human soldiers. These imaginary robots are usually **humanoid** robots – robots that are designed to look like humans. They are the same size and shape as people and have arms and legs, too. However, robots come in all shapes and sizes. While there are no humanoid robot soldiers yet, armies use many other types of robots, from mini tanks to flying **drones**.

Could this be what robot soldiers of the future will look like?

## Robots in warfare

Robots are moving machines capable of carrying out actions automatically, usually programmed by people using a **remote control** or a computer. Robots have been in use in the armed forces for many years. Many people trace the first use of military robots back to before World War II, when robots in the form of "teletanks" were being developed. These small, remote-controlled tanks were equipped with machine guns, flame-throwers and a smoke container that could be used to provide a **smokescreen**. The operator was in another tank that could be as far as 1.5 kilometres (0.9 miles) behind the teletank, and controlled the teletank using radio signals. Since then, many more advanced robots have been invented to help people carry out all kinds of military roles.

These World War II teletanks were called *Goliaths*. They carried explosives that could blow up tanks.

## The dangers of war

The advantages of using robots instead of humans on the battlefield are obvious. In wars, many people are injured and killed by guns, bombs and other weapons. These **casualties** and deaths are a price that many people are not prepared to pay, however inevitable a war may seem to be. Robots, on the other hand, are more easily replaced. In the heat of battle, robots are not scared so they may be able to react more quickly, and they do not experience feelings of anger or vengefulness that can cause even the best-trained soldiers to make mistakes. Many people believe military robots are the future of warfare.

## Robots are the future

Today, military robots are controlled by human operators, either nearby or at a distance. In the future, military robots might be able to act **autonomously**. This would completely change the face of warfare.

5

# Small bots

The robots most commonly used by the armed forces today are small, flat robots that run on caterpillar tracks, like those on a tank. These robots are designed to be able to ride over different types of land, including rough, rocky surfaces, or snow and ice. Depending on what they are designed for, they have different equipment, such as **sensors** or weapons, attached to their main body.

Caterpillar tracks give robots grip on all kinds of terrain.

## Tough and stable

These small robots are tough. They can fall off bridges and crash into things without being too badly damaged. Most are also designed to be **amphibious**. This means they can operate in and out of water, so they can drive through streams or deep puddles without stopping. The caterpillar tracks are made of a circular belt of ridged metal, which moves in a loop over the wheels. Caterpillar tracks spread the weight of the robot over a large area. So, instead of applying all the force on the small area where wheels touch the ground,

Many robots are operated using a handset like the ones you might use for a remote-controlled car.

treads apply it over the whole area of the track. This means a heavy vehicle is less likely to sink into the ground, or get stuck in snow or mud. Tracks also give a robot a large area of contact with the ground, which gives it very good grip and makes it very stable.

## Control

Many small robots are operated by a person using a joystick to control its movement, much as people use a joystick to steer a car when they play a computer game. Operators may also control a robot using a program on a computer. They can tap on the screen of a tablet computer to direct where the unit needs to go. Robots often have arms that controllers can use to lift or do things. They have cameras so that the operators can see what the robots see. Some robots can be controlled from only a short distance away, while others can be controlled from hundreds of kilometres away!

Some robots can have their treads modified to allow them to climb stairs without slipping backwards!

7

# Types of ground robots

Today, almost all military organizations use small military robots to perform some of the risky jobs that soldiers would otherwise have to risk their lives doing. Some are used to fire weapons, some to dispose of bombs and others for **surveillance** – to enter into enemy areas and spy on activities there.

*TALON* measures 86.4 cm (34 in.) long, 57.2 cm (22.5 in.) wide and is 27.9 cm (11 in.) high when its arm is folded away.

## TALON

*TALON* is a military robot that has been in use since 2000 and can be adapted to do different jobs. All *TALON* robots have camera and recording devices, and most also have a mechanical arm with a gripper at the end. *TALON* even has a microphone and a loudspeaker. *TALON*s have been used to get rid of live **grenades** and other dangerous explosives. Some *TALON*s have been equipped with sensors that can detect chemicals, natural gas, differences in temperature and **radiation**, so they can be sent to check areas that might be hazardous for human soldiers. Armies are also doing tests on *TALON*s to carry weapons, such as machine guns and rifles.

Most *TALONs* are used to save lives by disarming explosives that could harm human soldiers in action.

## Talented TALON

*TALON* moves slowly at speeds up to 6.4 km (4 mi.) per hour. It can climb stairs, ride over rubble, climb steep slopes and correct itself if it falls over. Its tools include things like wire-cutting tools for cutting through cables on bombs, and **X-ray** equipment for seeing through solid materials to find out what is inside. *TALON* runs on batteries and can work continuously for more than four hours before it needs recharging. It has seven cameras, which operators use to look all around it, to see where they want it to go and to watch out for danger. Operators drive *TALON* using a joystick remote control. The cameras can zoom in on objects, have night-vision capabilities and there is a **thermal imager**, which can "see" things that give off heat, such as people. These cameras have helped make *TALON* a good surveillance robot. It has been used to peer inside caves and other potential hiding places in remote places in the hunt for enemies. *TALON* robots are pretty indestructible. One has been blown up three times and after being fitted with new radio, cameras and sensors, it went straight back to work!

# Portable bots

There is a new kind of robot that is quickly becoming an important part of an army's equipment: the portable robot. These robots can be moved around because they are smaller, lighter and quick to set up and get started. They are being used to help soldiers on the front line in a variety of different ways.

## PackBot

*PackBot* is a series of lightweight, portable military robots with a video-game-style hand controller. Different tools and equipment, such as gripping tools and explosive-detection kits, can be attached to the basic *PackBot*, so it can be used for tasks including bomb disposal and hazard detection. *PackBots* have an extendable robotic arm that can stretch as far as 1.8 metres (6 feet) in any direction. This makes it easier to grab hold of difficult-to-reach explosive devices. It weighs fewer than 24 kilogrammes (53 pounds) so a soldier can quickly load *PackBot* into the boot of a Jeep, transport it to a site and carry it by hand to get closer to an operating position. It can be ready to use in under 2 minutes. *PackBot* runs on caterpillar tracks and has two flippers with small tracks that help pull it up slopes and over obstacles at speeds of up to 9.3 km (5.8 mi.) per hour.

*PackBot* is a light, but rugged, all-weather robot that is currently used by the United States Marines.

## Throwbot

At just 18 centimetres (7 inches) long, *Throwbot* is even smaller than *PackBot*. As its name suggests, this robot can be thrown into action! It is so tough that it can be tossed over walls or dropped from the air without breaking. *Throwbot* looks a little like a dumb-bell weight because it consists of a bar with a wheel at each end. After *Throwbot* has been thrown into potentially dangerous locations, such as confined spaces, buildings and tunnels, operators drive it using a hand-held control unit. The robot has a camera that feeds live images to the operator.

## Robots are the future

Robots such as *Throwbot* are fairly new. In the future they should be able to greatly reduce casualties because they allow commanders to see into potentially dangerous places and make sure they are safe before sending in soldiers.

Portable robots can be transported easily and operated from temporary camps, so they can be used any time and anywhere.

# Chapter 2

# Heavy-duty bots

Small and portable robots have their uses, but for some military jobs, brute force and strength are needed. This is when larger military robots are used. These heavy-duty robots are like trucks and tanks, but they have computers built into them, so they can be operated by remote control.

Bots allow soldiers to be safely out of harm's way during operations.

## Remote transport

The All-purpose Remote Transport System (ARTS) looks a little like a digger but without a driver. It was developed by the United States Air Force to remove or **disable** terrorist bombs from suspect vehicles or to clear landmines, while its operators and other soldiers were at a safe distance. At the heart of ARTS is a small commercial digger that has been adapted so that its steering equipment can be controlled by electric motors operated using radio control.

Cameras are mounted on the front and back, and on tools, to supply a video feed. Operators can control ARTS remotely and see what it is doing and where it is going from up to 4.8 km (3 mi.) away.

The front **articulated** arms can be fitted with a wide variety of attachments. These include:

- a high-strength steel digger bucket to dig up mines;
- motorized brushcutters to clear paths through vegetation so that soldiers can search for mines more safely;
- a charge setter so that soldiers can explode bombs and mines they find from a safe distance;
- a gripping robot arm that can handle large suspicious packages so an operator can investigate them.

# Robots are the future

Armed robotic vehicles (ARVs) are being developed that will eventually replace manned tanks in high-risk missions in the future. They are part of the United States Army's Future Combat Systems' robotic forces. ARVs will look and be used like tanks, but they will be controlled remotely by an operator located at a safe distance, either at a base or in an **armoured vehicle**. An assault version would carry weapons, such as anti-tank missiles, while a **reconnaissance** version would carry imaging and mapping equipment to assess enemy numbers and capabilities.

Combat bulldozer bots are often used to clear obstacles in areas where mines could pose a danger to soldiers.

# Robot dozer

The Armored Combat Engineer Robot (ACER) is a heavyweight among robots. It looks a lot like a bulldozer found on a construction site. ACER can be used as a transportation robot, to carry weapons, **ammunition** and other supplies for soldiers. It also uses its brute force to clear obstacles out of the way and it can be used to destroy landmines.

## Shifting debris

The main task of the bulldozer-like ACER is to use its might to clear roads and battlefields. In a war, roads may be blocked by damaged vehicles, fallen trees and other debris. ACER can have a bulldozer scoop attached to the front that collects and shifts debris. It also has a large mechanical arm above it to lift things out of the way.

ACER can be fitted with a huge cutting-and-grabbing tool, which is used to cut up and move debris that is too big to move in one piece. ACER weighs in at 2.3 tonnes (2.5 tons) and moves along at about 10 km (6.3 mi.) per hour. It runs on caterpillar tracks and can easily drive up steep slopes and over bumpy ground. It is operated remotely by one person using a control unit that has two joysticks.

ACER is fitted with steel armour-plating that can deflect bullets fired from a distance of 24.3 m (80 ft.) away.

## Tooled up

ACER can be fitted with various types of equipment, so it can be used for different jobs. Its mechanical arm can be used for lifting and disposing of explosives, and it can have a minesweeper attached to the front of it. Minesweepers are devices that scan for landmines buried just below the surface of a field or road, and then dig up and detonate the mines, making the area safe for soldiers and other people. When equipped with a special nozzle that sprays foam, ACER can also be used to put out fires after a bomb has been dropped.

Checking for landmines is dangerous. Robot minesweepers save many lives.

# Four-legged robots!

Most military robots run on either wheels or caterpillar tracks, but some can have four legs and walk! In 2014, the United States Marines trialled a four-legged robot called *Big Dog*. The official name for these robots was Legged Squad Support Systems, or LS3s. LS3s could walk so well that even if they were kicked from one side, they could still stay upright. They could carry up to 180 kg (396 lbs.) of equipment, weapons and supplies over long distances, across rough terrain.

LS3s were designed to be used to bring vital supplies, such as water, to places that army vehicles cannot drive to.

Having four legs made it easier for *Big Dog* to tackle rough ground like this.

## Big Dog

Like a faithful dog, *Big Dog* could follow soldiers wherever they went. It ran on a diesel engine and it could walk, run and climb for up to 32 km (20 mi.) before it needed refuelling, even while carrying heavy loads. It could walk through snow, muddy trails and across rubble.

*Big Dog* had four legs that were articulated like an animal's and it was the size of a large dog or small packhorse: about 1 m (3.3 ft.) long, 76 cm (2.5 ft.) tall and weighing 109 kg (240 lbs.) It had sensors that helped it detect large objects on the ground so it could go around them rather than bumping into them. *Big Dog* had an on-board computer, which was linked to another computer that its operator used. The controls were simple to learn and had joysticks. Even if the dog fell over, it was designed so one person could easily set it upright again.

## Robots are the future

*Big Dog* trials were, unfortunately, unsuccessful, as the robots' diesel engines were thought to be too noisy for use in battle. However, one day, if research resumes, quieter versions of these four-legged robots could be developed to accompany units of soldiers on missions. They would reduce the amount of equipment that fighters have to carry around, which can weigh more than 45 kg (100 lbs.)

# Chapter 3

# Underwater bots

Unmanned underwater vehicles (UUVs) are robots that can move and work underwater. For navies around the world, these vehicles free up sailors from dull, dirty and dangerous tasks. For example, many navies use human divers to clear dangerous mines and other obstructions, which threaten the safety of their own and other ships, seas and ports. UUVs designed to locate, identify and defuse such mines have made this important job much easier and quicker. They also avoid the need to put human divers' lives at risk.

Earlier underwater ROVs were towed on cables by ships at the surface.

## Bots past and present

Early underwater robots were remotely operated vehicles (ROVs). These unmanned bots were connected to a ship by a series of cables. They were designed with long, cylindrical torpedo shapes to make them **streamlined** to move through the water more easily. Many ROVs still work and look like this today. The cables transmit command and control signals between the operator and the ROV, allowing the vehicle to be driven from a distance. Modern ROVs may have a video camera, lights and articulated arms that can be used to pick up small objects, cut lines and attach lifting hooks to larger objects.

## Pluto Plus

*Pluto Plus* is an ROV designed to find and destroy underwater mines using a set of sensors that includes television cameras. It moves using electrical **thrusters** and is linked to a ship by fibre-optic cable or wireless link. It sends back information on its surroundings, and operators move it around using a remote-control console. It can dive to a depth of more than 300 m (985 ft.) and it can travel at about 11 km (6.8 mi.) per hour. *Pluto Plus* can also be used to secretly inspect suspicious ships while operators are far away from potential danger zones.

## Robots are the future

In the future, underwater bots could have such advanced sensors that they could easily swim around ports and harbours without bumping into rocks, ships, small boats and other things. This would mean they could be used to patrol ports and stop ships from bringing in goods unlawfully.

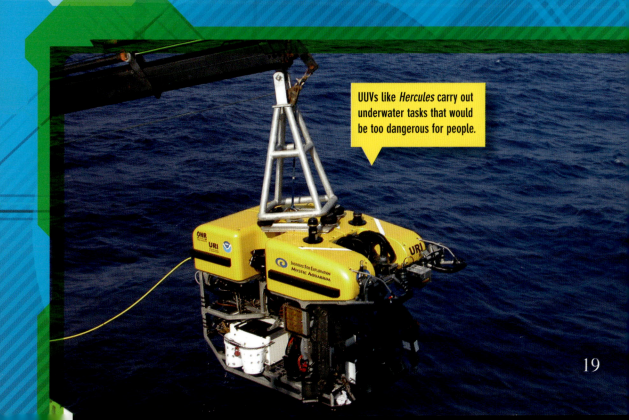

UUVs like *Hercules* carry out underwater tasks that would be too dangerous for people.

# Scorpio ROV

*Scorpio* stands for Submersible Craft for Ocean Repair, Position, Inspection and Observation. These large robots can be used to find and retrieve the wreckage of damaged naval ships and submarines, and they help locate and rescue survivors from sunken vessels.

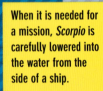

When it is needed for a mission, *Scorpio* is carefully lowered into the water from the side of a ship.

## State-of-the-art Scorpios

Like other ROVs, the latest *Scorpios* are connected to an operator on a ship. They have video cameras that provide full-colour images for the controller, and a set of strong lights that light up the deep, dark waters in which the robots move. They also have a depth-measuring system, tracking system and **sonar** with a range of up to 0.6 km (2,000 ft.) Sonar is short for Sound Navigation and Ranging and it is a system that uses sound waves to "see" in the water. A sonar machine sends out pulses of sound and then works out where something is from the time it takes for the echoes to be bounced back to the machine. The arms on *Scorpios* are very powerful. They can lift heavy weights and have several functions, including cutters that can cut through steel cable up to 2.5 cm (1 in.) thick. *Scorpios* come in different sizes, but they are all mid-sized bots. On average, *Scorpios* measure around 1.2 m (4 ft.) wide, 1.2 m (4 ft.) high and 2.4 m (8 ft.) long.

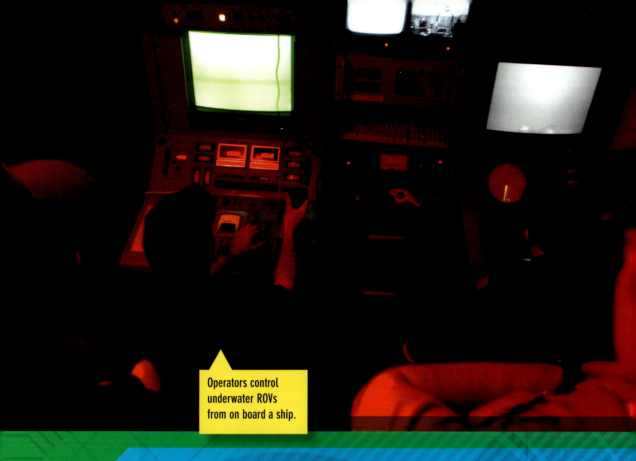

Operators control underwater ROVs from on board a ship.

## Rescuing people

*Scorpio* can be used to help rescue people from a submarine that has been hit in a battle, caught on a cable or stuck on the seabed. Once the submarine has been found, a *Scorpio* can be used to mark the site with beacons. If the submarine is tangled in something, the manipulator arm installed on the front of the ROV can be used to untangle the submarine. The manipulator can also clear debris from the submarine's escape hatch if it is blocked and stopping people from getting out. The ROV can also fit an underwater telephone for survivors to speak to rescue ships and can deliver life-support systems to a submarine in distress.

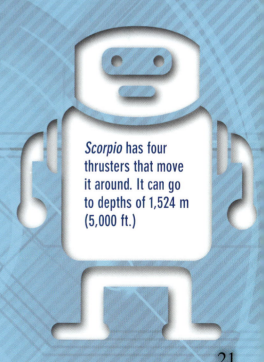

*Scorpio* has four thrusters that move it around. It can go to depths of 1,524 m (5,000 ft.)

# Hull Bug

One of the dull and dirty jobs that robots can do instead of humans in any navy is cleaning the hulls of ships. Over time, all ships and boats resting in water get a build-up of plants and small animals, such as sea grasses, barnacles and tubeworms, growing on their hull – the underwater portion of a ship. This is known as **biofouling** and it makes ships travel more slowly. In fact, biofouling can reduce a ship's speed by 10 per cent. Not only does this mean engines burn up to 40 per cent more fuel, which costs more money, but it could also mean a ship cannot get where it needs to in time, which could be a matter of life or death!

Cleaning the hull of a ship by hand is a dull, time-consuming job.

## Cleaning up

Cleaning off biofouling costs navies millions of pounds every year, but this could be reduced by using the *Hull Bug* robot. The *Hull Bug* is a type of autonomous underwater vehicle, or AUV, which means it is an underwater robot not connected by cables to surface ships. It runs on four wheels across a ship's hull, cleaning the ship's surface. The idea is for *Hull Bug* to be used frequently so that it can remove early traces of biofouling before it is solidly attached and too encrusted onto the hull. Regular cleaning is important because ships spend more than half their time in port, giving sea life plenty of time to grow on their hull.

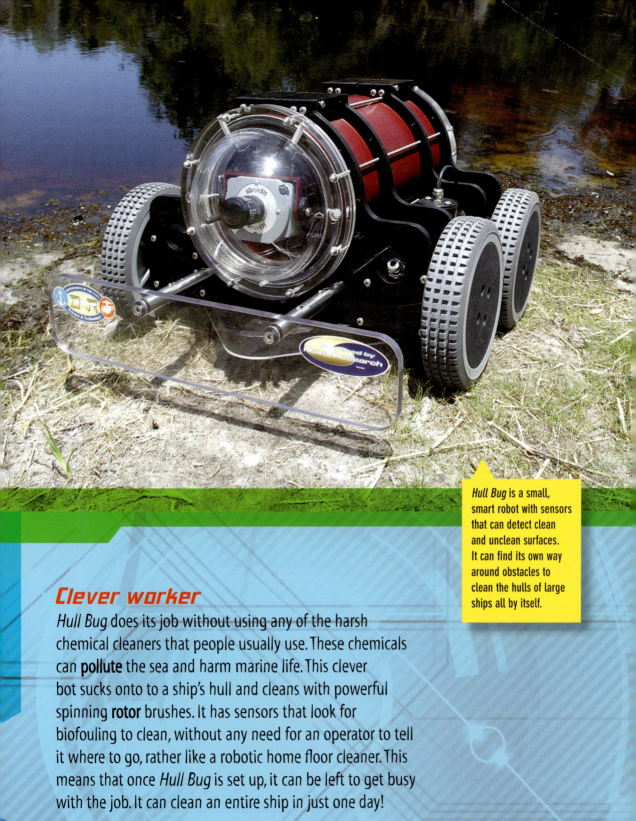

*Hull Bug* is a small, smart robot with sensors that can detect clean and unclean surfaces. It can find its own way around obstacles to clean the hulls of large ships all by itself.

# Clever worker

*Hull Bug* does its job without using any of the harsh chemical cleaners that people usually use. These chemicals can **pollute** the sea and harm marine life. This clever bot sucks onto to a ship's hull and cleans with powerful spinning **rotor** brushes. It has sensors that look for biofouling to clean, without any need for an operator to tell it where to go, rather like a robotic home floor cleaner. This means that once *Hull Bug* is set up, it can be left to get busy with the job. It can clean an entire ship in just one day!

# Robot navy

Armed forces have invented robot vehicles that can do dangerous jobs in place of people. These vehicles include boats that work above sea level, as well as under water.

Armed robot boats can attack enemy ships with less risk of losing human life.

## Robot boats

The United States Navy has been testing new robot boats. The Navy put a system called the Control Architecture for Robotic Agent Command and Sensing (CARACaS) into ordinary naval boats to see how they would work on a mission to protect a main ship against possible attackers. When the main ship was approached by a suspicious boat, the robot boats swarmed towards it and formed a defensive line between the boat and the ship they were protecting. The boats operated autonomously, without any direct human control, and they worked together. Radar readings from the boats were linked so that each boat's on-board computer could work out where the boat was in relation to the others. However, only a human sailor could order the unmanned boats to fire weapons.

Robot boats can operate on their own or as a group.

Some AUVs can dive to 3,048 m (10,000 ft.) and travel up to almost 130 km (80.8 mi.) without resurfacing.

## Echo Ranger

The *Echo Ranger* is an AUV shaped a little like a torpedo. It was designed to collect images of the seabed for the oil and gas industry, but now it is being adapted to patrol waterways for the US Navy and for surveillance operations deep underwater. It uses computers and sonar systems to collect and send information about what it "sees" back to a control station. If a number of these robots, and others like them, could be placed at different points on the seabed, navies could use them to track the movements of enemy submarines and spot vessels entering a region illegally. The advantage of larger AUVs like the *Echo Ranger* is that they house more equipment and carry out a wider range of surveillance activities.

## Robots are the future

The early success of robot boats suggests that in the future, navies and other military forces might be able to develop underwater robotic vehicles that could defend themselves or attack a hostile force.

# Chapter 4

# Flying mini-bots

Armies use several different small flying robots, mainly for reconnaissance. These are called unmanned **aerial** vehicles (UAVs) but they are more commonly known as drones. Many of these look like the model aircraft you might see flying in a park at the weekend, and they can be carried, launched and controlled by one person. Their flight is controlled either autonomously by on-board computers or by a pilot using a remote-control device on the ground or in another vehicle.

## Aerial surveillance

In the past, human pilots and crews have carried out aerial reconnaissance or surveillance. They fly over areas of land, such as enemy territory, looking for enemy troops and also for injured soldiers in search-and-rescue operations. The problem with using human crews is that it puts people's lives at risk and it also limits the time and therefore also the distance that can be covered — people need to return to base to eat and rest regularly. Having human crews also means that planes need to be bigger, so they use more fuel to fly than a drone would. Being bigger also means they are easier for enemies to spot.

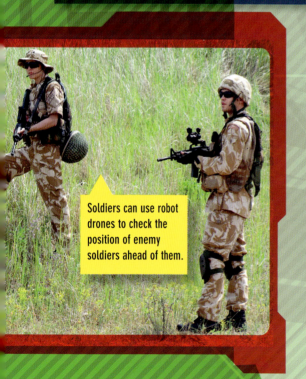

Soldiers can use robot drones to check the position of enemy soldiers ahead of them.

Drones can have a range as large as 800 m (0.5 mi.), a top speed of 35 kph (21.7 mph) and can fly for up to 30 minutes.

### Helicopter drones

One of the smallest drones in use is the *Black Hornet*, a tiny helicopter drone that measures about 10 cm (3.9 in.) by 2.5 cm (1 in.) and weighs just 16 grammes (0.6 ounces). This battery-powered drone is fitted with a tiny camera. It can fly unseen over enemy territory and send live video or images back to a hand-held computer, providing vital information to soldiers on the ground. The drone helps soldiers spot hidden fighters and explosives, and it can check whether open areas of land are safe before soldiers try to cross them. Soldiers can fly the *Black Hornet* using remote control or it can be programmed to fly autonomously. The great advantage of this pocket-sized robot is that its small size means it can fly through, below and between spaces and obstacles that most drones could not. It is also silent, so it can pass through confined spaces unnoticed!

Helicopter drones are so small they can fit in the palm of a person's hand.

# Kit planes

Drones as small as *Black Hornets* are not yet commonly used and also are quite delicate. Soldiers on the ground are more likely to be using a robust aeroplane drone that comes as a kit, made up of different pieces that can be assembled when they are needed. The advantage of this type of UAV is that it can be transported easily, so soldiers can bring it with them and use it wherever their patrol goes.

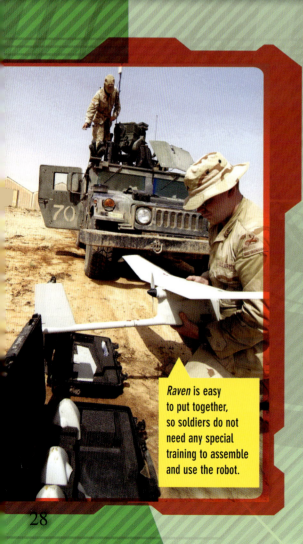

*Raven* is easy to put together, so soldiers do not need any special training to assemble and use the robot.

## Flight of the Raven

*Raven* is a UAV made up of separate parts that fit into three small cases, which in turn fit into a backpack. *Raven* is easy to assemble and can be ready to use in minutes. To launch it, a soldier simply has to throw it into the air, much as you would a paper aeroplane. If it is spotted and there is a danger it might be shot down, the operator can instruct this drone to return to its launch point immediately by pressing a single button. *Raven* lands by hovering just above land and then dropping down, and does not need a stand or base to return to. This means it can take off and land just about anywhere, which is vital for a troop of soldiers on the move. *Raven* can be programmed to follow set routes autonomously, using **GPS** technology, or operators can control its route from the ground.

Soldiers throw *Raven* into the air to send it on a mission.

*Raven* can fly for an hour or longer before its batteries need to be recharged.

## Day and night images

*Raven* weighs about 2 kg (4 lbs.) This lightweight robot has a variety of cameras that send live images and detailed information back to the operator. Some send live colour images and others have **infrared** cameras. These cameras detect infrared, or heat energy, and convert it into an electronic signal, which can then be turned into a thermal image on a screen. Thermal images show coloured shapes of things that give off heat. They can show where enemy soldiers are at night or if they are hiding.

29

# Copying nature

When humans first invented aeroplanes they looked to nature for inspiration. They studied the flight of birds and insects, such as dragonflies, to see how the shape of their wings helped keep the insects in the sky. Inventors of the *Samarai* flyer modelled their robot on the way maple seeds spiral down through the air when they fall from a tree.

Designers of flying robots often look to nature and the way insects, like this dragonfly, fly for inspiration.

## The Samarai *flyer*

The *Samarai* is a tiny, single-rotor (blade) helicopter that glides in the same way as a maple or sycamore seed. This lightweight bot weighs fewer than 227 g (8 oz.) and is just 40.6 cm (16 in.) long, so it can easily be stored in a backpack. *Samarai* has only two moving parts: it has a disc-like unit that contains its battery and electronics, and a single wing with a **propeller** mounted at the far end. When it flies, the whole drone spins around in a circle, with the disc at the centre. An adjustable wing flap allows operators to steer it.

*Samarai* can be launched from the ground, when it lifts itself straight up into the air like a helicopter, or thrown by hand like a Frisbee. It is ideal for military missions in towns and cities because it can fly both indoors and outdoors. It can fly both up and down, as well as sideways. Like a helicopter, it can also hover at one level to film its surroundings. The tiny camera it carries rotates at the same speed as the drone's body. Special stop-motion video software cancels out the rotation so that the operator can see a steady stream of clear images with a 360-degree view. *Samarai* can be used for surveillance and reconnaissance missions. Soldiers can throw it to see around a corner or over a building to check if there are any enemies there.

*Samarai* can fly for only about 30 minutes, but designers hope to improve on this so it can be sent on longer missions in the future.

The *Samarai* flyer got its name from the word "samara", which means "winged seed". This robot's entire body spins as it moves through the air.

### 3D printing

Another amazing thing about this mini flying bot is that it was built using 3D printing technology! Small layers of plastic were printed and put together to create a single form. Using a 3D printer means *Samarai* can be produced quickly and cheaply, and one day it may be adapted to different missions or to carry weapons.

# Chapter 5

# Robot air force

In the modern armed forces there is a new type of pilot. These pilots may have never felt the **G-forces** that press on the body when flying at high speeds, or feared their fighter jet being shot down by an enemy plane. Their aeroplanes may fly on missions that take them far from their base, but these new pilots never leave the ground. They operate a variety of normal-sized planes using a computer.

*Global Hawk* uses **satellite** links to **communicate** with its portable ground control station.

## From autopilot to no pilot

Pilots on manned aircraft have been using something called autopilot for a long time. Autopilot is a system that frees pilots from having to physically use their hands on the controls. This does not mean that pilots can have a nap while their planes are in autopilot! A normal plane cannot fly itself. Autopilot just helps pilots by controlling certain aspects of a flight, such as speed, engine power and following a route. Only new robotic planes, such as *Global Hawk*, can really be counted as planes that can fly themselves.

## Global Hawk

Steered by a pilot using a computer mouse, *Global Hawk* can fly over long distances, stay in the air for 32 hours or more, and carry up to 680 kg (1,500 lbs.) of gear, such as scientific equipment. It flies at heights of around 15,000 m (50,000 ft.), which is much higher than the **altitude** at which commercial airliners usually fly. It is 4.5 m (14.8 ft.) high, more than 13 m (42.7 ft.) long, and has a **wingspan** of more than 35.4 m (116 ft.) It is powered by a single Rolls-Royce engine and made from aluminium, graphite composite materials and some fibreglass. *Global Hawk* has a variety of sensors that enable it to provide surveillance and reconnaissance information, for example, to locate targets for air-strike missions, in any weather, day or night.

*Global Hawk* can record detailed intelligence, surveillance and reconnaissance data.

## Robots are the future

*Global Hawk* can fly higher than manned aircraft, so it can fly high above storms. This means it can provide us with information about dangerous weather, such as hurricanes, which could help make more accurate storm predictions in the future.

# Drones at war

Some flying drones are used in times of war to locate enemy targets and fire weapons against them from the air. *Reaper* and *Shadow* are two such drones.

Each *Reaper* drone is operated by a team of two and can fly high above the ground.

## Reaper

*Reaper* is a drone that can be used for surveillance missions and also for air strikes. It is about the same size as a small business jet with a wingspan of 20 m (66 ft.) It can fly at 470 km (292 mi.) per hour at altitudes of up to 15,240 m (50,000 ft.) Each drone is remotely controlled by a pilot and a sensor operator at base, via satellite link. The pilot flies the plane, and the sensor operator uses its different sensor systems, including infrared and **night vision** cameras, to spy or locate targets. *Reaper* can be fitted with different equipment, depending on the mission. For example, it can carry both weapons and surveillance equipment, or be armed with four Hellfire missiles and two 226-kg (500-lb) **laser**-guided bombs, which rarely miss their mark and can even hit moving targets.

## Shadow

*Shadow* is a robot aircraft that can be used for reconnaissance, surveillance and target acquisition. It can transmit images in near-real-time during day or night and in bad weather. It provides commanders with a bird's-eye view of the battlefield and as well as being used to drop bombs, it can also drop medical supplies to precise locations. *Shadow* can locate, recognize and identify targets up to 125.5 km (78 mi.) away from the operations centre. What large robot planes like *Shadow* cannot do is take off and land just anywhere. *Shadow* is launched by regular wheeled take-off on a runway or from rails on a special, wheeled trailer that flings it into the air. To land, it comes down onto a runway and is caught by a tail hook.

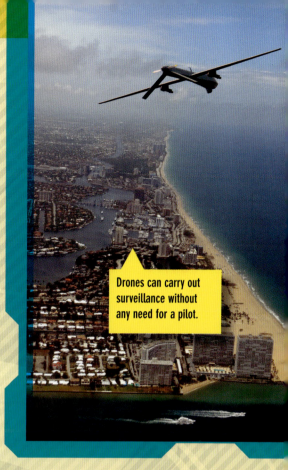

Drones can carry out surveillance without any need for a pilot.

## Robots are the future

In the future, people believe most bombings and aerial attacks could be carried out by drones based on robot aircraft, such as *Reaper* and *Shadow*, working autonomously, rather than being controlled by humans. Some people say this will not happen because making military decisions about whom to kill should remain the responsibility of humans.

*Shadow* can stay in the air for around eight hours before it needs to find a runway to land.

# Predator

*Predator* was the first of the robot aircraft to carry weapons, and this unmanned aircraft system (UAS) is also the one that has been used most in combat. *Predator* is a high-tech aircraft that can take part in reconnaissance and combat missions in times of war. It can also support troops on the ground in dangerous conflicts, while being controlled by a crew far away from the front line. The *Predator* drone has advantages over human pilots because it reduces risk to human crews and can stay in the air much longer than humans can.

## Predator *stats*

*Predator* looks a lot like a normal plane with a two-blade propeller at the front. It is 8.2 m (27 ft.) long and 2.1 m (6.9 ft.) tall, with a wingspan of 14.8 m (48.6 ft.) It can fly at altitudes of up to 7,600 m (25,000 ft.) and travel at a maximum speed of 217 km (135 mi.) per hour.

*Predator* prepares for take-off!

*Predator* can travel up to 643.7 km (400 mi.) from its ground station. The crew that controls *Predator* includes a pilot to steer the aircraft and command the mission, someone to operate sensors and weapons, and a mission coordinator, who ensures the team knows what the overall battle plans are. The crew operates *Predator* from inside the ground-control station via a line-of-sight data link or a satellite link when it goes out of sight.

*Predator* can stay in the air for up to 40 hours without having to stop.

## Predator's *payload*

A **payload** is the equipment and weapons an aircraft carries. *Predator* carries missiles and a variety of equipment and sensors, including a Multi-Spectral Targeting System. This advanced system for viewing the ground below includes an infrared sensor, colour or black-and-white daylight television camera, an all-weather radar that produces images of targets, and laser lights that can pinpoint targets. These systems help *Predator* drones accurately locate and target enemies, while minimizing the number of **civilians** who are injured or killed. *Predator* drones also help soldiers on the ground by sending them detailed visual intelligence about the location of the enemy. As it can "see" in bad weather, it can even help soldiers navigate their way through sand storms in desert warfare.

# Unmanned fighter

The X-47B robot fighter plane is the first unmanned aerial vehicle designed to take off and land at sea. This futuristic-looking fighter drone can take off from and land on an **aircraft carrier** on the ocean. When an ordinary plane takes off from an aircraft carrier, a crew member on the ship signals to the pilot inside to tell them when to take off. X-47B is different. The signal is given to an operator on deck, who simply presses the launch button on a controller strapped to their arm to send the robotic aircraft flying off the front of the ship.

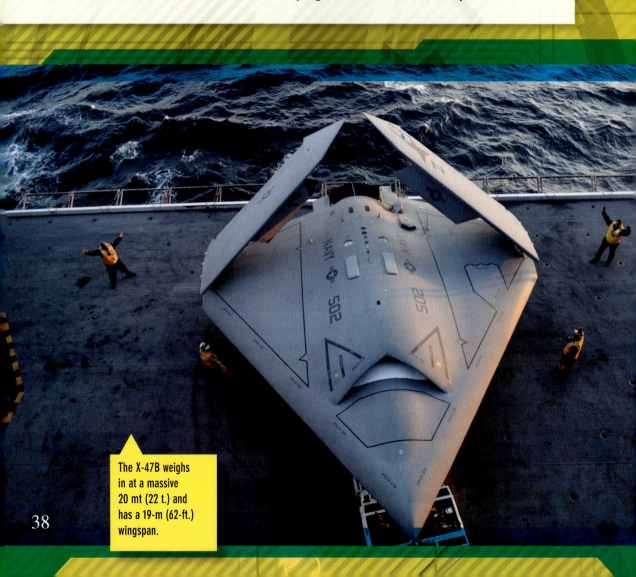

The X-47B weighs in at a massive 20 mt (22 t.) and has a 19-m (62-ft.) wingspan.

## Battles from the sea

There is an important advantage to launching planes from aircraft carriers at sea. It allows aircraft like the X-47B drone to be used around the world without needing permission to take off from airfields in other countries. The X-47B is suitable for war missions launched from aircraft carriers because it has folding wings and it is built with materials not easily damaged by salt water. It also has a wireless remote-control device that moves it around crowded flight decks without it teetering off the edge.

## Flight controls

The X-47B is designed to fly autonomously, following orders from the operator to an on-board computer. For example, it might be given a target to look for or a weapons factory to bomb using its full-sized weapons. Once it has its instructions, X-47B is able to use **artificial intelligence** to think for itself, plotting slight changes to its course, depending on readings it takes using technology such as GPS, autopilot and collision avoidance sensors, unless a mission operator needs to step in.

## Robots are the future

The **prototypes** of X-47B that are being tested have a range of around 3,200 km (1,988 mi.) and can stay in the air for a maximum of about six hours. In the future, newer versions of X-47 may be programmed to refuel themselves while they are in the air (with fuel transferred from another aircraft) so they will be able to complete much longer missions and travel greater distances. This would give the navy around-the-clock surveillance and targeting capabilities.

# Chapter 6

# Robot soldiers

There are no robot soldiers in any armies in the world ... yet. However, inventors have developed robotics equipment that human soldiers can wear to help them in battles.

Many films and games feature robot soldiers such as this one, but they are not yet used in real battles.

## Robotic exoskeleton

One example of technologically advanced robotics equipment is an **exoskeleton** worn over a uniform to increase strength, agility and stamina. The battery-powered robotic suit contains a built-in micro-computer, controllers, sensors and motors called actuators. The actuators make the exoskeleton move with the soldier and help the soldier lift and carry heavy objects. Soldiers on the ground often have to carry heavy loads that tire them out and can lead to injuries.

This soldier is wearing an Integrated Soldier System. The camera with zoom that is mounted on the barrel of the rifle could help to make every soldier a marksman.

The robotic exoskeleton has limbs made of a strong, lightweight metal called titanium. The limbs help take the weight of heavy loads so the soldier does not have to, allowing them to carry another person on their back or use a front attachment to lift a weight of around 90 kg (200 lbs.) hundreds of times without getting tired. The suit is also flexible enough to allow the soldier wearing it to crawl, climb or run while carrying heavy loads.

## Integrated soldier systems

Another type of robotic suit under development is the integrated soldier system (ISS). An example of an ISS is the *Land Warrior*. An ISS consists of a computer, a radio, a rifle and a helmet-mounted display eyepiece — all of which are linked electronically. The rifle has a camera that allows soldiers to view targets up close so they can even see and shoot around corners when they hold out the rifle. Soldiers control the whole system and can transmit voice, data and images to other soldiers and to commanders, without taking their hands off the gun. For example, there are buttons for radio communications, for taking and transmitting pictures, and for calling up maps on the helmet-mounted display, which has moving icons that show where the soldier and other troops are. There are many advantages to an ISS like this. For example, it will allow soldiers to track each other's location without using voice radio or hand signals.

In a war zone, ISS can see movement inside buildings and is able to identify both enemy and friendly troops.

# Robot guns

Robot guns, or remote weapons systems, are computerized units that are linked to a weapon such as a machine gun. They can be attached to the top of a vehicle to help the soldiers inside the vehicle locate and lock onto targets with more precision. As well as improving a vehicle's ability to find and destroy targets, the other advantage of systems such as these is that soldiers can use them to fire weapons from a safe position inside an armoured vehicle, rather than having to stand above it. Other robot guns are used in defence to locate and destroy weapons sent to blow up ships or land stations, such as military command bases.

## CROWS

The United States' Common Remotely-Operated Weapons Station (CROWS) is a system of guns and sensors that can be mounted on the top of different smaller armoured vehicles, such as Humvees. It contains a daytime camera, a thermal (heat-sensing) camera and a laser rangefinder, which can pinpoint targets using laser light. The devices are controlled from inside the vehicle using a joystick and screen. These devices can find a target at long distances and while a vehicle is moving. The weapons CROWS carries have a larger ammunition supply than similar weapons, so they need reloading less often. This means the crew can stay inside the vehicle where they are safe for longer.

CROWS is attached to an armoured vehicle. Its operator can locate and shoot at targets while inside the vehicle.

## Phalanx

The Phalanx Close-in Weapon System is a robotic gun system that automatically tracks and destroys anti-ship missiles that have passed all other ship defence systems. Anti-ship missiles are guided missiles (bombs steered by radio signals) that are designed for use against ships and large boats. Phalanx has computers, a forward-looking infrared sensor and a radar to guide the gun, which is mounted on a swivelling base. The radar is used to search for and locate missiles, decide if they are a threat and then track and fire at them. A land-based version of Phalanx has also been used to protect bases from incoming rockets and other missiles. Phalanx is a complete unit that can be fitted to a ship. This makes it ideal for smaller ships which may have fewer sensors and less sophisticated targeting systems than large military ships.

The Phalanx Close-in Weapon System can shoot at a rate of about 75 rounds per second.

Missiles can target and sink large ships. Phalanx tracks and destroys these missiles.

# Military robot future

Some people believe that the robotic systems we already use, which are made up of a human operator and a robotic unit, give us the best of both worlds. They give armies the benefit of human decision-making with a unit that can be repaired if it is shot at or blown up. However, technology is advancing faster than ever and it may not be long before there really are humanoid robot soldiers fighting our battles.

## A robot soldier?

*Atlas* is an example of the kind of robot soldier we could see in the future. This life-size robot walks on two legs, which leaves its hands free to lift, carry or fire weapons. It is strong and coordinated enough to climb using its hands and feet. *Atlas* can also negotiate most spaces, from rough outdoor landscapes to crowded streets.

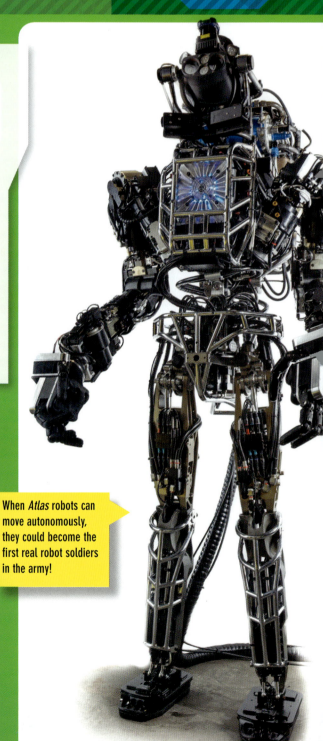

When *Atlas* robots can move autonomously, they could become the first real robot soldiers in the army!

*Atlas* has articulated hands containing sensors that will be able to use tools, which only humans can currently use. Its head contains stereo cameras and a laser rangefinder. At the moment it is slow and powered by electricity that it receives through a long cable, so it cannot go far.

In the future it is expected that robot soldiers like *Atlas* will be able to walk freely without their systems of cables and tubes, and as technology advances, they will be able to follow a variety of orders after they have been programmed to do so. There could be advantages to this. Fewer human soldiers would be killed if robots took their place in battles. A human soldier's emotions may sometimes make them behave recklessly, while robots would always follow orders precisely. Robot soldiers could also be much less expensive than a human army.

# Robots are the future

There are many advantages to using robots in the army, but some people still question whether robot soldiers could ever really replace human soldiers. They worry that robots could malfunction and start shooting at anyone. Robot designers say this is highly unlikely. Robots usually rely on human operators and in the unlikely event that a robot with a gun did go out of control, operators could shut it down simply by pushing a button. Some people believe robot soldiers are **unethical** and that it would be wrong to program machines to kill. What do you think?

45

# Glossary

**aerial** in the air

**aircraft carrier** military ship that has a large deck where aircraft take off and land

**altitude** height of something above the level of the sea on Earth's surface

**ammunition** objects, such as bullets and shells, that are fired from weapons

**amphibious** able to operate on land and in water

**armoured vehicle** vehicle with a protective metal covering

**articulated** having two or more sections connected by a flexible joint

**artificial intelligence** capability of a machine to copy intelligent human behaviour

**autonomously** able to control itself, not operated by a person

**biofouling** build-up of living things, such as plants, on a surface in the water

**casualty** person who is injured or killed in an accident or war

**civilian** person who is not in the armed forces

**communicate** to share or exchange information

**disable** to stop something working

**drone** robotic aircraft

**exoskeleton** rigid external covering for the body

**G-force** force of gravity on a moving object

**GPS** (Global Positioning System) electronic tool used to find the exact location of an object

**grenade** small bomb that can be thrown by hand or launched mechanically

**humanoid** shaped like a human

**infrared** rays of light that cannot be seen by human eyes

**laser** very narrow beam of highly concentrated light

**night vision** describes devices that help us to see at night

**payload** total amount of equipment and people that can be carried by a vehicle

**pollute** make something dirty or unsafe

**propeller** set of rotating blades that provide the force to make an aeroplane or boat move

**prototype** first working model of a new invention

**radar** device that uses radio waves to find out the position of an object

**radiation** rays of energy given off by radioactive elements

**reconnaissance** act of studying or watching a place or enemy to find out information about them

**remote control** device used to operate a machine from a distance

**rotor** part of a machine that turns around a central point, such as a helicopter blade

**satellite** electronic device placed in orbit around Earth, used to gather and send information

**sensor** device that detects changes, such as heat or movement

**smokescreen** cloud of smoke created to conceal military operations

**sonar** system that uses sound waves to find and calculate the location, size and movement of underwater objects

**streamlined** designed to move easily and quickly through air or water

**surveillance** keeping watch on or observing someone or something

**thermal imager** device that makes images of things we cannot see by sensing the heat they give off

**thruster** engine that moves a vehicle or robot through water by shooting out a jet of fluid in the opposite direction

**unethical** not morally correct

**wingspan** total length of an aircraft's pair of wings, from tip to tip

**X-ray** invisible ray of light that can pass through an object to see inside it

# Find out more

## Books

*Fighter Aircraft* (Ultimate Military Machines), Tim Cooke (Wayland, 2015)

*iRobot* (Augmented Reality), Clive Gifford (Carlton Books, 2016)

*Special Forces* (Heroic Jobs), Ellen Labrecque (Raintree, 2013)

*Weapons and Warfare* (It'll Never Work: An Accidental History of Inventions), Jon Richards (Franklin Watts, 2016)

## Websites

Discover more about the robots and other equipment used by the British Army:
**www.army.mod.uk/equipment/23256.aspx**

Meet some more robots that are inspired by nature at:
**www.bbc.co.uk/newsround/36343502**

For a fun introduction to robots, check out:
**www.sciencekids.co.nz/robots.html**

# Index

aircraft carriers 38, 39
amphibious (vehicles) 6
armed robotic vehicles (ARVs) 13
armies 4, 8, 10, 13, 16, 26, 40, 44, 45
Armored Combat Engineer Robot
   (ACER) 14, 15
artificial intelligence 39
ARTS 12, 13
*Atlas* 44, 45
autonomous underwater vehicle
   (AUV) 22, 25
autopilot 32, 39

*Big Dog* 16, 17
*Black Hornets* 27, 28
bombs 5, 8, 9, 10, 12, 13, 15, 34, 35,
   39, 43

cameras 7, 8, 9, 11, 13, 18, 19, 20,
   27, 29, 31, 34, 37, 41, 42, 45
caterpillar tracks 6, 10, 15, 16
Common Remotely-Operated
   Weapons Station (CROWS) 42
computers 4, 7, 12, 17, 24, 25, 26,
   27, 32, 33, 39, 41, 43
Control Architecture for Robotic
   Agent Command and Sensing
   (CARACaS) 24

drones 4, 26, 27, 28, 30, 31, 34–35,
   36–37, 38, 39

*Echo Ranger* 25
exoskeleton 40, 41
explosives 5, 8, 9, 10, 13, 15, 27

Future Combat Systems 13

G-forces 32
*Global Hawk* 32, 33
*Goliaths* 5

helicopter drones 27
*Hull Bug* 22–23
humanoid 4, 44

information 19, 25, 27, 29, 33
integrated soldier system (ISS) 41
intelligence 33, 37

kit planes 28–29

*Land Warrior* 41
Legged Squad Supports Systems
   (LS3s) 16

mechanical arm 8, 14, 15
micro-computer 40
mines 12, 13, 14, 15, 18, 19
minesweepers 15
missiles 13, 34, 37, 43

navies 18, 22, 24, 25, 39
night-vision 9, 34

operators 4, 5, 7, 9, 11, 12, 13, 17,
   18, 19, 20, 21, 23, 28, 29, 30, 31,
   34, 38, 39, 42, 44, 45

*PackBot* 10, 11
Phalanx Close-in Weapon System
   43
pilots 26, 32, 33, 34, 35, 36, 37, 38
*Pluto Plus* 19
portable robots 10–11, 12
*Predator* 36–37

*Raven* 28, 29
*Reaper* 34, 35
reconnaissance 13, 26, 31, 33, 35, 36
remote control 4, 9, 12, 27
remotely operated vehicles (ROVs)
   18, 19, 20–21

robot boats 24, 25
robot soldiers 4, 40, 44, 45

*Samarai* 30, 31
satellite 32, 34, 37
sensors 6, 8, 9, 17, 19, 23, 33, 34, 37,
   39, 40, 42, 43, 45
*Shadow* 34, 35
ships 18, 19, 20, 21, 22, 23, 24, 38,
   42, 43
sonar 20, 25
submarines 20, 21, 25
Submersible Craft for Ocean
   Repair, Position, Inspection and
   Observation (*SCORPIO*) 20–21
surveillance 8, 9, 25, 26, 31, 33, 34,
   35, 39

*TALON* 8, 9
tanks 4, 5, 6, 12, 13
teletanks 4, 5
*Throwbot* 11
thrusters 19, 21

unmanned aerial vehicles (UAVs)
   26, 28
unmanned underwater vehicles
   (UUVs) 18, 19

video 10, 13, 18, 20, 27, 31

weapons 5, 6, 8, 13, 14, 16, 24, 31,
   34, 36, 37, 39, 42, 44
wheels 6, 11, 16, 22
World War II 4, 5

X-47B 38, 39
X-ray 9